A PICTORIAL H
OF KINGSBR
AND THE SURROUNDING AREA
[from the Cookworthy Museum Collection]

Compiled by
Sue Linton
Photographic assistance
Sharon Wellington

ORCHARD PUBLICATIONS
2 Orchard Close, Chudleigh, Devon TQ13 0LR
Telephone: (01626) 852714

ISBN 1898964 60 2

Printed by
Hedgerow Print, Crediton, Devon EX17 1ES

Contents

Introduction

Kathy Tanner established the Cookworthy Museum Photographic Collection and in 1988 published 'Around Kingsbridge in Old Photographs'. This new book shares with a wider audience more of the fascinating collection of photographs now held in the Cookworthy Museum Public Access Database. With over 4500 photographs scanned and more to come, there is plenty of choice. The photographic database is available for the public to examine, to order copies or to add photographs and information to the collection. If I have missed out any village or hamlet in the area it is almost certainly because there are no relevant photographs in the Cookworthy Museum database to date. We will always welcome further additions to our collection. I hope you enjoy looking through this book as much as I enjoyed compiling it.

Acknowledgements

Many thanks to all the people who have helped in this compilation, including David Barnwell, Bill Blank, Mike Bullar, Lyn Collins, Jackie Corder, Malcolm Darch, Geoff Dickenson, Esme Edwards, Nicola Fox, Reg Hannaford, Winifred Harwood, Stuart Hext, Judy Leathart, Anne Lidstone, Rob Linton, Margaret Lorenz, Alwyn Milburn, Cliff Peach, Frankie Pearce, Steve Salter, Betty Squire, Jeanne Stoggall, Jack Tanner and Sandra Westlake. They have all provided information or technical help at some point, and of course, encouragement.

Copyright thanks to: Judges Postcards Ltd, (01424 420919) - references: P0655, P0493, P0494, and P0495, Western Morning News and Arthur Reed [P1497.1]

KINGSBRIDGE

Kingsbridge, the market town for the area, was originally two towns – Kingsbridge, which was set up by the Abbot of Buckfast in the 13th century, and Dodbrooke, which was named in the Domesday survey of 1086. Kingsbridge was centred around Fore Street, Dodbrooke around Church Street. Each had their own market, church, portreeves and town officials, but after several hundred years the two towns were amalgamated in 1893.

SOUTH VIEW OF KINGSBRIDGE, FROM THE ESTUARY.

An early etching of Kingsbridge, south view from the estuary, dated 1818. [P1504.2]

Kingsbridge estuary 1880, with logs seasoning for use in shipbuilding. Leighton House in the background [now part of Harbour House]. [P0693.1]

Victorian drinking fountain, built to celebrate Queen Victoria's Diamond Jubilee – useful to horses and dogs in its heyday. The stone base is now in the grounds of Quay House, but the fountain itself is lost. Trant's mill dominates this view of Kingsbridge. [P0836.2.6]

The Quay area in 1930s. Ryeford Garage, on the left, was started after the First World War by John Perkins, with support from Major Stapleton-Cotton, then of Dodbrooke Manor [they served in the same regiment during the war]. It began life in an ex-army Nissen hut. The Anchor Hotel, now the Quay, has remained largely unchanged from the 1880s. Stear's Bakery was jointly owned by the two daughters and one son of Stear the saddler in Duke Street. The stone bollards near the head of the creek were removed every summer to make room for the fair. [P1403.21]

Squares Quay and Boon's Cottage, on the West Alvington side of the estuary, pre 1881. Twyford House, now Quay House, visible in the background. As part of the Ilbert estate, this quay was closed for one day every year to make the necessary distinction between it and the other quays. [P0303]

View across the estuary from West Alvington Quay, pre 1881, showing Quay Cottage, Victoria Place and logs seasoning on Dodbrooke Quay. Most sea trade berthed here until New Quay was built. [P0304]

Britton's Corner, showing Shillabeer's butchers at the corner of Mill Street, which later became Donovan's butchers, and was destroyed by bombs in 1943. Also showing the private houses of the rich tradesmen. At this time, the commercial centre was at the top of the hill, around the Shambles, and this part of Fore Street was mainly residential. [P1403.15]

Fore Street north of junction with Duncombe Street, with the old fire station on the right. The Kingsbridge branch of Devon County Library was based above the fire station until it moved to the Town Hall. The Liberal Club was next door. [P0203]

Toll gate at the top of Fore Street. All toll gates in the Kingsbridge area were dismantled in 1884. [P0026]

Photo of painting of church and Shambles, 1830. The clock is on the end gable of the church as the Town Hall was not built until 1850. One theory for the blank face on the clock is that the church clock did not need the face as it was completely hidden by the tower, and the clock design was not changed when it was put on the Town Hall in 1875. It is actually an access door to allow internal maintenance of the clock. [P1403.10]

Fore Street during the 1870s, looking down from the Shambles. Britton's tailors is at the bottom, and in the centre distance is Tacket Wood Quay, which served the local quarry. [P0766]

Fore Street and Shambles in the 1880s – little change to this part of Fore Street. The White Hart Hotel [now The Bed Expert] is on the left [with a swinging sign] and the little shops to the right are now the Spar shop. These show clearly the gradual encroachment of many shopkeepers, starting with a temporary stall on the pavement, which would gradually acquire a temporary, then permanent awning, until the shop frontage could simply be built on, sometimes with the upper stories being extended as well. [P0554]

Fore Street in the 1930s, looking uphill. Midland Bank, now HSBC, on the left and the current site of Woolworths (bombed in 1943). Green the saddler and Tiddly Brown were there before that disaster. Note that traffic was two-way at that time. [P0366]

White Hart Hotel in 1904, with Browns shoe shop on left and the entrance to White Hart Passage on right. Note the sign is different from that in the 1880s. [P0200]

Albion Hotel, built 1874, photographed in 1910-1912. Steere's shop is now Belinda David. [P0746]

Perrott's saddler's shop circa 1890 – situated next to Baptist Lane, where Alan's Apple now is. Perrott's were at 26 Fore Street from 1861 to 1977. [P0499b]

Stewart, Dispensing Chemist, 56 Fore St. This shop was a chemist as long ago as 1841, as Balkwills, and from 1934-1979 Boots the Chemist. A. E. Fairweather was trained at Stewarts before moving to his own business in Salcombe. The Cookworthy Museum has an extensive collection of glass plate photographs taken by him. [P1416.9]

Hoskings, haberdashers of Church Street, circa 1930. In 1939, Percy Hosking, draper, was listed as trading at 9-11 Church Street. [P1154]

G. Moysey's shop in the 1930s, at 19 Church Street. G. Moysey, father and son, were based in Church Street from 1878. [P0517]

Looking west to Fore Street. The cottages on the left have since been demolished and the site is now the fire station. Otherwise, little has changed in Duncombe Street since this photo was taken circa 1900. Roger's Dairy Farm was on the right behind the low wall. [P0751]

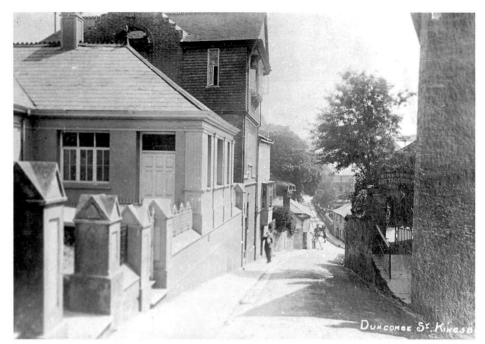

Duncombe Street. The Masonic Lodge on the left has undergone several extensions over the years – here the entrance is at the side, just below the steps to Richmond Terrace. To the right of the picture is the entrance to the Cottage Hospital, set up in 1898, which moved to its current site on Plymouth Road in 1928. The mortuary at this hospital was a small building at the bottom of the garden, with 'I am He that liveth and was dead. Behold, I am alive for evermore, Amen' [Revelations 1:18] written on the wall above the mortuary slab. [P1345]

Bond's Quay circa 1895 – Barquetine about to be towed out by steam launch. The remaining buildings of the army barracks, built in 1804 for the Napoleonic Wars, are visible on the hill. They were designed to house 600 men. [P1403.23]

The Crabshell Inn at Bond's Quay, with sailing boat Bertie beside quay. New Quay Inn, now the Crabshell, was set up by the Bond family in the 1840s to satisfy seamen's thirsts. [P0373]

New Quay, more popularly known as Bond's Quay, as the Bond family owned it for several generations, circa 1844. [P0822]

King of Prussia circa 1904, with Perry Spear's corn and grain merchant building in the centre, which was bombed in 1943. Stear's the saddler on the right corner and Harry Hayter's sweetshop, the half-tiled building. To avoid the appearance of being unpatriotic, the name of the pub was changed to George Inn during the two world wars, although there is a theory that it was actually named after a famous 18th century Cornish smuggler, John Carter, nicknamed the King of Prussia and based at King's Cove [also known as Prussia Cove] near Penzance, Cornwall. He and his six brothers controlled the area for a good forty years, and their business was documented in the autobiography of John's brother Harry, who converted to Methodism and turned his back on smuggling, but was careful not to implicate his family. [P0637]

Recreation ground in the 1950s, with palm trees covering the area which is now a miniature golf course. The trees were removed in the 1960s. The houses in Derby Road are visible in the background. The entire recreation ground was reclaimed from marshland after the First World War as a memorial. [P0809.2]

THEN. Tumbly Hill, a steep lane between Ropewalk and Squares Quay, and popular with carriers trying to avoid paying tolls at the turnpike at the foot of West Alvington Hill. [P0836.8.2]

AND NOW. Tumbly Hill/Kiln House in 1999. The cottages have been demolished and replaced with retirement apartments. [P1537.27]

Quay circa 1900. View east to weighbridge and current Harbour House. Grants coal store, later Shinners, on the left where Quay Garage is at present. The passage by Leighton House [in centre background] led to Balkwill's Coal Store, while his office was in the round building to the left. [P0841]

Combe Royal, a private mansion, then a nursing home, now Social Services offices. Was offered for sale in 1876 with seventeen acres, at an asking price of £6,250. [P1389.21]

Kingsbridge, circa 1890, from Belle Hill, looking over Welle House [demolished and replaced by retirement apartments] towards St Edmund's Church. The tower of All Saints Church, West Alvington, can be seen on the horizon. Welle House was an ancient seat of the Champernowne family, who owned much of Dodbrooke for generations. There is a legend that a monk's passage runs from Welle House to Dodbrooke Church. The stone arch, which is all that remains of the old house, is still in use in the current building. [P1431.2]

SALCOMBE

Until the mid 19th century Salcombe was mainly a fishing and trading port, but the arrival of the railway at Kingsbridge boosted the growth of tourism. Salcombe grew from small fishing village into a major fishing and shipbuilding centre for the area, but now is mainly a sailing and holiday centre.

Salcombe harbour, town, Bar and Bolt Head, looking south west. [P0656]

Harbour from East Portlemouth side, showing Chants' boatyard, early 20th century. [P1041]

Salcombe town from Ilbertstow [now Snapes] Point [P1400.2.3]

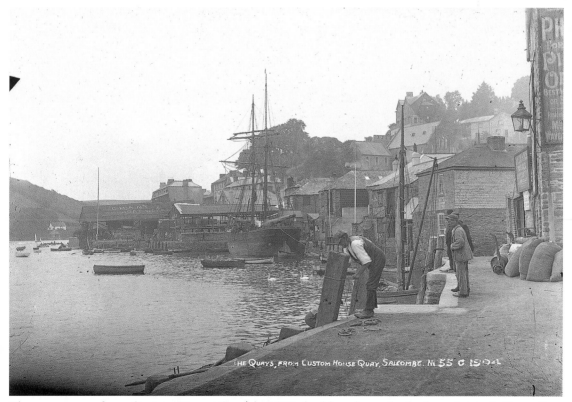

The quays seen from Custom House Quay in 1904, looking down the harbour towards Council
Quay [now Whitestrand] and the boatyards. [P1400.2.5]

THEN. Custom House Quay with paddle steamer Ilton Castle, circa 1900. [P1400.1.18]

AND NOW. Custom House Quay, 1999. [P1537.42]

The Pier End, showing Cliff House Gardens and the Ferry Inn. [P1400.2.2]

Circa 1900. Looking down Fore Street towards the church. Shipwrights Arms on the left, Lloyds Bank left foreground. Signboard for Gunn's Temperance Hotel. A modern post office was built on the site of Gunn's Cafe, which was destroyed by a World War II bomb. The post office then moved to the corner of Courtney Street, and ironically the current post office is now housed in the Shipwrights Arms. [P0009]

Bottom of Fore Street looking towards Union Inn [now Fortescue Inn], 1908. Giles the baker and Trute the plumber on the left, and on the right a boot repairer, baker [now the Upper Crust], and N. Marsh & Co Steamer and Railway booking office – Salcombe maintained a railway booking office until 1961. [P0116]

Union Inn, Fore Street, showing steps to Buckley Street. [P1400.5.4]

Island Street, with Island Terrace right foreground, and a Wesleyan chapel [no longer existing] at the junction. Mr Fairweather, the photographer, obviously felt the need to remind the children not to move! [P1400.4.21]

Island Street, circa 1910. Horse [Prince] and refuse cart. [P1400.5.2]

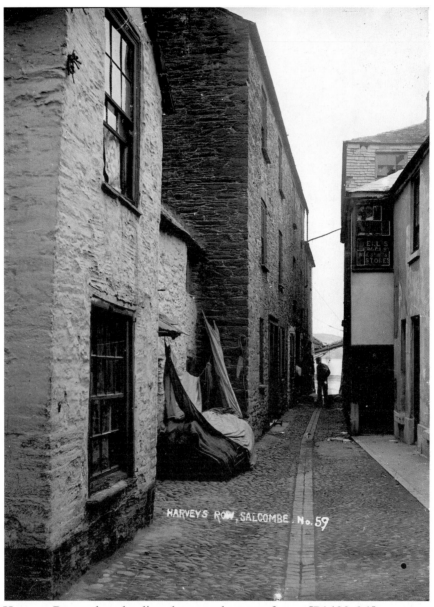

Harveys Row, a lane leading down to the waterfront. [P1400.6.1]

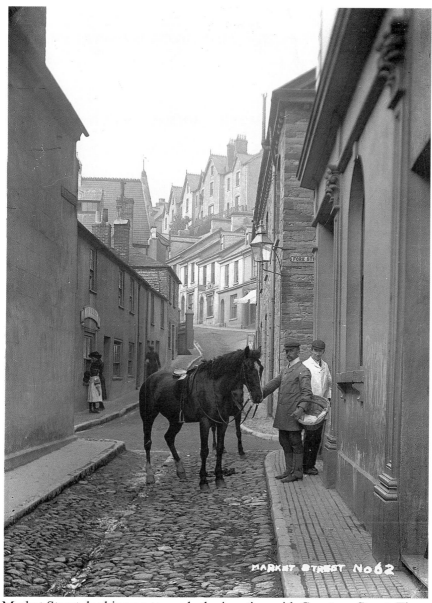

Market Street, looking up towards the junction with Courtney Street. The delivery man in the white coat is Dick Lapthorne. [P1400.4.3]

The Court, Breakwater Bay, 1920. The four cottages on the right were destroyed by a bomb in World War II. On the left is the site of the Salcombe Day Centre. [P0127]

Buckley Street pre 1906. The glazed porch left of centre was the first post office in Salcombe, in 1821. The kitchen of the cottage on the left was the first meeting place of Methodists in Salcombe, in 1814. [P0150]

Ferry Corner, Fore Street, at the top of Ferry Steps circa 1900. A dog rests on the steps of what is now Dusters Bistro. [P1046]

Robinson's Row, off Fore Street, circa 1900. [P1056]

Church Hill, pre 1947, looking west uphill to the church. Dr Vincent Twining is on the left. The 12th-13th century cottage in the centre was pulled down and replaced in the mid 1920s. [P0082]

Post office staff, pre 1911, in front of the Fore Street post office include Jack Ford, Mr Butler [the postmaster], W. T. Murch and George Ash. [P0216]

View down street in Chivelstone, with the church tower at the end of the row. [P0474]

Chillington. The house with centre group of people became the post office. [P0874.3]

Stokenham. The thatched barn in the foreground is now the car park for St Michael and All Angels Church and the Church House Inn. [P1158]

Tradesmen's Arms, Stokenham. [P0655]

View up Church Lane to Slapton Church, circa 1950. [P0809.9]

Slapton pre 1925. [P1416.5]

Sherford, circa 1948. [P0825]

Cottages on village green at East Prawle. [P0565]

Torcross. View from the top of the cliff. [P0649.3]

Torcross circa 1912. [P1488]

Start Bay Inn, Torcross circa 1900. [P0836.14.4]

Washing on Beesands beach – when not used for the Monday wash, these lines were used to dry fish for bait. [P0077]

Beesands 1930. [P1398.19]

Beesands. View north along the road circa 1950s, the post office and phone box on left. [P0809.8]

Beeson village main street – post office on the right. [P0645.3]

View north up Hallsands main street, 1896.   [P0836.19.3]

Hallsands pre 1914. [P0471]

HALLSANDS AFTER THE DREDGING.   J. R. Gill, Kingsbridge.

Hallsands between 1914 and 1917 showing the drop in the beach level after the dredging. [P0916]

Hallsands. Looking north by the temporary bridge over chasm after one of the more devastating storms, possibly 1902. Note the man with crabpot standing outside the Prettyjohn house. [P0731]

Prospect House was built in 1923, quite literally, by the Trout sisters, particularly Patience and Ella, who dug the foundations, channelled the water supply from a spring, and handmade 8000 blocks before handing the rest of the building work over to Mr Perrott, of Kingsbridge. Originally intended as a guest house for friends, it proved so popular that it became Trout's Hotel, eventually closing in 1959. It is now luxury holiday apartments. [P0641.2]

South Pool circa 1880. At the bottom of the village near the bridge. South Pool was owned by the Heles family and its descendents for generations, but was sold in 1911 to pay the newly introduced death duties. Until 1949, there was no mains water or electricity supply to the village. [P0621b]

South Pool circa 1890. [P1353.2]

South Pool. View of bridge over the creek, circa 1910. [P1484]

THEN. West Alvington, circa 1900. Nine chimney pots on the centre house, one hundred years later there were still seven pots there. The road seems wider than now - without the raised pavement it probably was! West Alvington was an independent village in the 19th century – villagers could live, work and shop in the village, using Kingsbridge as a market town. [P0895]

AND NOW. West Alvington, 1999. [P1537.37]

Malborough pre 1909. [P0121]

Bolt Head Hotel, South Sands and lifeboat house [built 1878] from the north. The lifeboat house closed in 1930 as the Salcombe-based lifeboat took over responsibility for the area. [P0796.3]

Lower Batson. View from Salcombe harbour of Lower Batson with boats on the mud and allotment gardens on the right. [P0798b]

St Andrews Church, South Huish. Inconveniently placed for its parishioners it was abandoned by 1866 and allowed to fall into ruins upon the building of Galmpton Church. Much of the church was re-used elsewhere in the area. The altar table, chalice and paten went to the Hope Cove Chapel. The 15th century chancel screen to a private chapel at Bowringsleigh and the stone pillars to make up the north arcade in St Thomas of Canterbury's, Dodbrooke. The four bells and 14th century font went to Galmpton. [P1003]

Holy Trinity Church, Galmpton, built 1866-7 to replace South Huish. The Salcombe doctor, pony and trap, circa 1905. [P0959]

Outer Hope village. View from clifftop to north, 1898, showing coastguard cottages. [P0961]

Inner Hope, looking down into the square. [P0661]

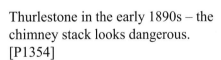

Thurlestone in the early 1890s – the chimney stack looks dangerous. [P1354]

The Moult and Bolt Head, Salcombe. [PO403.2]

Bantham from the Ham, looking north up the river. Boatsheds and boats on the beach below the village. [P0313]

Bigbury-on-Sea from Burgh Island. [P0494]

Burgh Island from the cliffs at Bigbury-on-Sea – before the hotel was built in 1929. [P0381]

Burgh Island Hotel – water bus crossing. This particular water bus was apparently designed and built at Okes' Garage, Kingsbridge. [P0493]

Panoramic view of Bantham, Burgh Island, Bigbury-on-Sea and Stoke Point circa 1965. [P1431.21]

St Ann's Chapel, Bigbury. A medieval cell is now incorporated into the Pickwick Inn, shown here circa 1907. There is a tradition that Royalists used to meet in the upper room during the Civil War. Another dangerous looking chimney stack. [P1367.4]

Ringmore circa 1950. [P0280]

Woodleigh post office pre 1912 – closed 1971. [P0577]

Loddiswell, circa 1900. Looking down the street, Yalland's grocers on left. Child front centre was later a housemaid at Kingsbridge Grammar School. [P0574]

Fore Street, Loddiswell. [P1524.3]

Well Street, Loddiswell, circa
1910. [P0580]

Aerial view southwest of Churchstow in 1960, before the development of housing estates to the south. [P1409]

Aveton Gifford, Steeres Kings Arms Hotel circa 1910. Until recently, this was the Ebb Tide Hotel, and is now the Fisherman's Rest. [P1378.1]

Fore Street, Aveton Gifford, circa 1920. Left to right: Gertie Sanders, Syd Clarke in pram, Mrs Sibley carrying Stan, Edie Moore, Syd's mother, Mrs Rimmer and Mrs Clarke. [P1369.4]

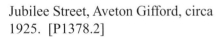

Jubilee Street, Aveton Gifford, circa 1925. [P1378.2]

Main street in Aveton Gifford, with the general store on the right, now closed. The opening of the by-pass, while improving Fore Street by reducing traffic, led to the closure of one of the general stores in the late 20th century, and the remaining store closed recently. [P0675]

Churchstow circa 1900, view east down street. Post office on right, the church on left – little change except that no-one would dare to stand in the street nowadays. [P0589]

Broad Street, Modbury, at the bottom of the hill in 1907. An omnibus with solid tyres is waiting outside Trinick, painter and stationer. Modbury was within the Kingsbridge Union area, so its homeless folk were sent to Kingsbridge workhouse. [P1367.3]

Broad Street, from the top of the hill, 1930. [P1367.2]

Pre 1917 view of seafront road, Hallsands, looking towards Start Point. Some men are making crab pots while sitting on sea defence wall. Crab pots here were woven from the reeds of Slapton Ley, which were also used at that time for thatching as they were very durable. Crabs were shipped live to Southampton in a crab smack every two weeks or so for the luxury liner trade, and also by the early morning train to London until the closure of Kingsbridge Station in 1963. [P0431]

Hallsands, pre 1900. Various members of the Login and Prettyjohn families – Philip Prettyjohn was at this time the landlord of the London Inn, a building which he left in 1900, feeling it to be unsafe. He was quite right, and his family moved further up the cliff path to the only house which continued to be habitable after the storm of 1917. [P0643]

Jack King of Kingston weaving crab pots, which were baited with fish stuck down the funnel on hazel twigs. The pot was then weighted with stones and placed on the sea bed. The growth in the crab industry came as the pilchard industry declined. [P1431.17]

Peter Birley Hurrell and his younger brother Henry, on the beach at Outer Hope, circa 1927. They worked the fishing boat 'Olive' until 1929 when Peter went to sea with his son, then aged fifteen. At that time he was second coxswain on the Hope Cove lifeboat Alexandra, and his son was the youngest member of the crew. [P1384.1]

Good catch of grey mullet at beach below Trouts Hotel, 1940. [P0880.2]

Seine fishing at beach below Trouts Hotel, Hallsands, 6 May 1940. When a shoal was spotted from the top of the cliff, the men would launch the seine boat and row around the shoal, casting a net to encircle it. Men, women and children on the beach would then haul in both ends of the net with its catch. The best would be sent to Kingsbridge for onward transmission to the London markets, and the rest shared out and kept for local use. [P1496.3]

Folly Farm, Bigbury circa 1925. Man working a three-horse drawn reaping machine. [P0286.4]

Folly Farm, Bigbury circa 1925. Mr Hooppell made a record of many of the farming methods and tools which were disappearing from use. Here he shows a man and horse-drawn farrow. [P0286.13]

Farming at Malborough. Two shire horses pulling a balance plough, which turned one furrow at a time. This design was popular because it left very little headland around the fields, making maximum use of the land, and, using the mouldboards, laid all furrows the same way. One of the last farm implements made specifically for use with horses. [P0634]

Threshing at Aveton Gifford, using a steam engine. This type of traction engine travelled from farm to farm and needed about a dozen men to operate it. One of the biggest local contractors of threshing machines in the early 20th century was William Yabsley, based at Goodshelter, East Portlemouth. He adapted the machinery at Waterhead mill for use in his ironwork, making implements from locally-mined ore. [P0687]

Croft Farm, West Charleton, threshing machine. [P0723]

Cornish's Farm, East Charleton circa 1956. Horse-drawn reaping machine, a late use of horses in farming. In the 1890s, East Farm, run by the Cornish family, was considered a good example of small-scale farming. [P0786.3]

Tractor-drawn mechanical reaper at a farm near Bigbury-on-Sea – three men were needed. One to drive the tractor, one to operate the reaper, and one to follow on foot to rake up. [P0820.1]

Flax farming in West Charleton between 1927 and 1937. The plants were grown close together to maximise their height [which could top twelve feet] and therefore the length of the fibres. The stems were pulled by hand and soaked to release the fibres. [P0638.8]

Flax farming in West Charleton, 1927-1937. The plants were then left to dry for several weeks – a successful flax harvest needed weeks, not days of dry sunny weather. Here the flax fibres are hanging to dry under Mrs Caldwell's supervision. This type of flax fibre was used as a substitute for hemp in rope-making but presumably proved uncommercial. [P0638.14]

Men hoisting hay – starting to build a hayrick using a pole. [P0957]

Harvesting near Salcombe using a three-horse-drawn reaper, 1900-1910. The attendant dogs are waiting to catch the rabbits as they are chased out by the reaper. [P1416.8]

Harvesting at Pond Farm, Aveton Gifford, using a horse-drawn reaper, and with plenty of children in pinafores to help, circa 1900. [P1431.12]

Dodbrooke market in Church Street, originally weekly, became monthly in the 18th century, and finally merged, on the same site, with Kingsbridge market in the 19th century. There were plenty of complaints from the residents in Church Street and Ebrington Street that the market was badly sited and should be moved, but the market remained here until a new site was built at Ropewalk in 1922. [P0555 and P0556]

A South Devon farm wagon was specially designed to cope with steep hills, narrow lanes and awkward bends, so had to be light and manoeuvrable, with small front wheels which pivoted under the wagon bed. [P0490.9]

Cider press at Batson Hall Farm, Batson, 1985. [P0908.1]

Thatching a cottage at Bottom Road, Galmpton, circa 1905. [P0285]

James Steere Woodmason, basket maker of Dukes Mill, Aveton Gifford. Third generation of basket makers based there. Born 1876, died 1965, having started to learn his craft at the age of twelve. He grew osiers in marshy areas to make willow baskets of varying sizes [some of which are in the Cookworthy Museum]. The willows were cut in February, stacked in a stream until April and then pulled through hand-made shears and placed in the sun to whiten and dry before being woven into baskets. [P0177f]

Sketch of limekiln – either at Salt Mill Quay or Tumbly Hill on the opposite bank. By the 17th century, limestone from Berry Head, Plymouth and further afield supplied the limekilns in the area. [P0907]

Kingsbridge Estuary.

Date's Boatyard. William Date launched his first ship in 1847. Kingsbridge's only boatyard, Date's built over eighty five vessels between 1837 and 1912. At its peak, it employed forty men. However, Kingsbridge could not compete with Salcombe and East Portlemouth for the number of ships built. [P0851.3]

Washabrook Mill, Dodbrooke. [P0680]

Trant & Sons lorry in 1962, laden with flour and inching its way out of the mill and into Mill Street – an extremely tight fit! [P0632.5]

The staff of Trant's Mill, Kingsbridge, 1900. Originally a corn mill built in the 13th century, it was converted to making woollen cloth in 1798, and re-converted to a corn mill in 1845. It closed down in 1967 and was demolished in 1984. Photo includes A. P. Trant, P. Trant, and Mr Perraton. [P0035]

Kelland's Brewery, Church Street, Kingsbridge, just below the London Inn. Left to right: Arthur Kelland, William Stephen Arthur, John Kelland, John Creber, George Rundle. [P0189.1]

Lidstone's Foundry, the largest of several in Kingsbridge. Most houses in the area had a Lidstone range in the kitchen. Lidstone's began making agricultural tools in 1739, and in the 19th century made most of the metal fittings for Date's ships. In 1920 it was taken over by Burgoyne, and examples of both Lidstone and Burgoyne ironwork can be found around Kingsbridge. A Lidstone range was even discovered in Newfoundland. The foundry was destroyed in one of the bombing raids in 1943. This group of workers in Lidstone's Foundry includes a father and son. [P0754]

Facing page. Raymond Muggeridge, blacksmith at Moreleigh until 1982. He was the fourth generation blacksmith in his family, the second to be based at Moreleigh. Tools made during his apprenticeship are now in the Cookworthy Museum. At least one farmer, in the Woodleigh area, used to take his horses to the local blacksmith, a mile away, and leave the horses to make their own way home when the blacksmith had finished with them. [P1438]

Interior of Stokenham forge before its clearance in 1990, showing the vice, anvil, cauldron and various tools. Many of the tools are now in the Cookworthy Museum. [P1380.15]

Rake Quarry, Loddiswell, 29 March 1930, showing Mr and Mrs Northcott in the centre with their employees and a few friends. [P1448]

Elijah Pearce, builder, decorator, carpenter and undertaker. In 1889 he was based at Church Steps, Fore Street, Kingsbridge and by 1895 at 119 Fore Street, where the business operated for at least forty four years. [P1450.1]

Boon coachbuilding workshop at the head of the estuary on Squares Quay in the late 19th century. John Boon was listed in trade directories at Square's Quay in 1870. In 1890 both John Boon, coach builder, and Edward Boon, carriage builder, were at Square's Quay, but in 1902 only Edward was still in business. [P0928]

The interior of Hanger Mill, North Sands, which provided the water supply for Salcombe until 1954. [P0341]

Pamela Bond, char at Woodleigh Rectory, who died in 1906. Doing the washing chore beside the shrubbery, perhaps for the photographer's convenience, using a tub made of stave construction, circa 1900. [P1310.1]

The Dartmouth to Kingsbridge coach nearing Kingsbridge along Embankment Road circa 1912, showing the unmade road surface and pavement. [P0021]

Dartmouth to Kingsbridge coach ready to depart from Torcross, circa 1907. The stagecoach service began soon after the road along the Slapton Line was opened in 1856, and by 1880 ran eighteen coaches a week. An extra horse was always added at Torcross to cope with the steep hill at Strete Gate, on the way to Dartmouth. The service was suspended in 1916 when Lewis Guest the

coachman went to war. The loss of the coachman, and shortage of horses due to army demands made the service untenable. It was re-started after the war, with Lewis Guest again as the coachman, but closed in 1924. Lewis then became a carrier around the local villages. [P1430.4]

Horsedrawn mailcart with driver travelled between Salcombe and Kingsbridge. This photo was taken between 1910 and 1922, when the service ceased. [P0435]

Richard West, Loddiswell carrier, outside 99 Fore Street, Kingsbridge, with his wagon drawn by a pony and a donkey, circa 1900. [P0581]

Donovan's horse-drawn delivery van in Church Street, Kingsbridge. Donovan's was in Church Street in 1878, and moved to its current address in Fore Street in 1893. It is the longest established family business in Kingsbridge, now in its fourth generation. [P0721]

Photo for Messrs E. & B. R. Noyce, charabanc proprietors, taken in Loddiswell circa 1925-1927. Their advertising jingle:
'If a trip you want in moderation
You need have no hesitation
For we have the reputation
Of the local population.
Bring along your deputation,
We will discuss the situation
And you can choose your destination.' [P1433.5]

THEN. Entrance to Kingsbridge railway station, circa 1900. [P0222]

AND NOW. The site of the entrance to Kingsbridge railway station, now an industrial estate, in 1999. [P1537.5]

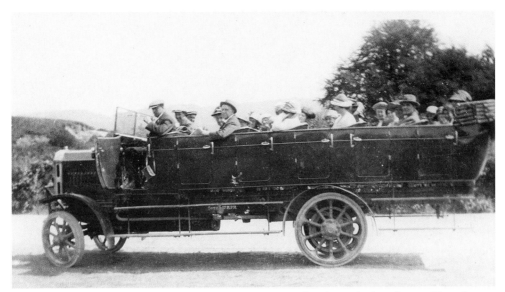

Charabanc in June 1921. The chassis is that of the first lorry belonging to Trant's Mill with the seating part made purposely to be added when necessary. The lorry was used to fetch wheat and deliver flour. Driver Ernie Lane was one of the office staff at the mill for many years. [P0254]

Loddiswell Station, situated near Woodleigh, with a steep climb of nearly a mile up to the village of Loddiswell. This station was never as popular for trips into Kingsbridge as GWR had hoped. The villagers tended to use the rival bus service which went through Loddiswell itself. [P0488]

Kingsbridge Railway Station, shortly before opening day,
on 18 December 1893. A railway to Kingsbridge had been
wanted for many years, but arguments over the route and
problems with financing meant that it was not built until
the end of the great railway boom. It closed in September
1963 under the notorious Beeching axe. A group of local
town councils were negotiating to buy the line and run it as
a tourist attraction, but came out of the initial meeting with
British Rail to find the contractors already tearing up the
lines. [P0214]

View along Kingsbridge platform as passengers board a steam train, circa 1914. The
man in the foreground carrying a stick and looking at the camera is Robert Morrison
Carter, miller of Shindle Mills, Bowcombe. [P0322]

General view of Gara Bridge station taken from the east, overlooking the line with the river Avon and bridge on far side and Harts Wood in the background. [P1425]

Thatched boatyard barns at Bantham, circa 1939. There is now a larger boathouse on this site. [P1367.7]

Ilton Castle on its maiden voyage between Kingsbridge and Salcombe, 21 February 1906. Salcombe Town Band is on the foredeck. [P0433]

Paddle steamer passing Tacket Wood circa 1925. [P1403.26]

Rowing boat ferry service between Salcombe and East Portlemouth. [P0707a]

The first Salcombe-East Portlemouth motor ferry in 1911, the King George V, commanded by S. W. Ryder. [P0126]

Vessels unloading in front of Bond's Quay, including the steamer 'Express', which was built by J. Hurrell in 1885, seen here letting off steam. New Quay Inn, now the Crabshell, set up by the Bond family to cater to seamen's thirsts, in background. New Quay was built as the head of the estuary silted up, at the point where the deep water channel came close to the eastern bank. Before then vessels came right up to Dodbrooke Quay at the head of the estuary, or Salt Mill Quay, near the present recreation ground. [P0926]

Salcombe lifeboat, Sarah Anne Holden, in harbour between 1916 and 1925. [P1068]

Wreck of sailing barque 'The Lady Young' at Bigbury Bay in October 1879. Burgh Island in background. The crew were all rescued by breeches buoy, but the steward died after falling from the rescue 'chair' onto the rocks. The barque, at 598 tons, became a total loss. [P1413.4]

Belgian steamer 'Charles Jose' of Antwerp ashore on Slapton Sands 11 December 1933. It was refloated a week later. [P1497.1]

The SS Jebba, a passenger liner from Sierra Leone, which ran aground on rocks off Bolt Tail on 18 March 1907. Conditions were too dangerous for the passengers and crew to abandon ship, or for the rocket apparatus to be launched from the cliff, so Isaac Jarvis and Jack Argeat, of the Hope Cove lifeboat crew, climbed the 200ft cliff, manhandled the equipment to sea level and rigged up a bosun's chair. This saved 117 of the 155 people rescued, and earned the two men the Albert Medal [the modern equivalent is the George Cross, the highest civilian honour in the UK]. [P0988.2]

The awards presentation for the rescue operation of the SS Jebba, at Hope on 24 May 1907. [P1522]

Schooner Ensign wrecked on Blackstone Rock, Salcombe, on 31 January 1915. [P0990]

Start Point lighthouse was originally built in 1834, and was enlarged in 1871-1874. This view taken pre 1904, looking south east. [P0476]

Captain Date, captain of 'Lizzie'. [P0703a]

Schooner 'Lizzie', 111 tons, built 1872 by Date's of Kingsbridge. Captains: W. Sheriff, W. F. Date. Lost at Teignmouth on 12 February 1909. 'Lizzie' was owned by Hingston & Co. [P1013]

Elsie Adams, nee Blake, a talented violinist and leader of the Kingsbridge Operatic Society orchestra, who, with her pupils, gave an annual concert for many years. The museum holds programmes from 1901 to 1953. In 1922 she married E. C. Adams, also a violinist, and they continued the concerts. From 1916 to 1933 the proceeds went to the Cottage Hospital, and in 1948 to the Kingsbridge War Memorial Fund. [P0206]

Mr Blake, a piano seller of Kingsbridge, and the father of Mrs Elsie Adams. [P1085]

Miss Frances F. Luscombe [Flossie], a teacher at Twyford School. Her father was a carpentry teacher at Kingsbridge Grammar School until it moved to Westville in 1931. Born circa 1897, Frances Luscombe was educated at Twyford School, and studied at home and in Paris. She was a teacher in other parts of England before returning to Kingsbridge and Twyford School in 1943. She remained with the school when it was amalgamated with the Grammar School in 1944 until her retirement in 1961. [P0904]

Mr and Mrs Luscombe, the parents of Frances Luscombe. Mr Luscombe worked at Pearce's, and taught carpentry at Kingsbridge Grammar School in the 1920s and early 1930s. [P0899]

W. H. Squire, 1871-1963, a noted cellist and composer, whose first public performance was in Kingsbridge Town Hall in 1879 at eight years of age. In 1937 he performed in Westminster Abbey at the coronation of King George VI. Pupil at Kingsbridge Grammar School 1878-1880. The W. H. Squire music prize is still presented by the Kingsbridge Community College Trust. [P1376r]

A studio portrait of handbell ringers – thought to be six brothers - Jack, unknown, Albert, George, Bill and Joe. [P1509]

Elizabeth Prettyjohn, born in 1884, the last full-time resident of Hallsands. She remained in the family house halfway up the cliff when the rest of the villagers were forced to abandon their homes in February 1917. With no mains water or electricity, it was a tribute to her toughness that she only left the house shortly before her death in 1964. The house is still standing, and used as a holiday home, although the cliff path has become increasingly dangerous in recent years. [P0156]

Miss Margery Ilbert of Bowringsleigh, a great benefactor of the village of West Alvington and a stalwart supporter of the Women's Land Army in the Second World War, she was a generous friend of the Cookworthy Museum in its early years. Died 1984. [P1401.1]

William R. Gay started Hillside School for young gentlemen in Ebrington Street in the mid 19th century, and later took over Mr Pearce's school in Fore Street. A noted amateur photographer and, as this photograph suggests, a talented painter, he was responsible for the figures of the apostles painted on the chancel screen at St Thomas of Canterbury's Church, Dodbrooke. [P0764]

George Steer, blacksmith at New Quay, with some of the tools of his trade, circa 1885. One of his sons [Sidney] trained as a chemist, another [George Vincent] as a printer. [P1089]

S. R. STEER, Kingsbridge, S. Devon.

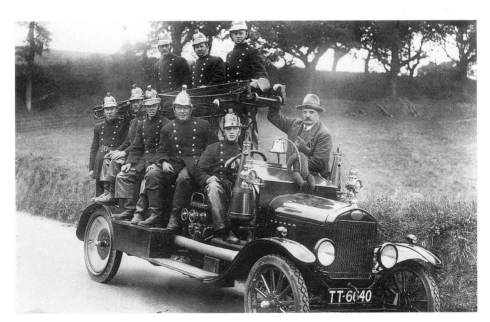

Fire brigade 1929. Back row: Jack Sparkes, Mr Tucker, Donald Rowe. Front row: Mark Overy, Jim Camp, Captain George Cope, Charles Hill. Mr Edey, the superintendent is in civilian clothes and wearing a trilby. A local joke at the time claimed that the Ford engine had to be pushed up Tacket Wood hill! [P0787]

William Baton, a seaman of the 'Kingsbridge Packet' until he lost his right leg. His wooden leg was subscribed for by Constitutional Club members. He became a miller, and fattened pigs for Lidstone Butchers. [P1404.15]

Pre 1912. Five men on a wall outside the site of the yet to be built Links Hotel, Thurlestone. Back row: Joshua Boyd [in charge of building the Links Hotel], Edward John Tanner [clothier], Langworthy [butcher], unknown, William Stubbs [employed by boot factory in Northampton and in this area on business with E. J. Tanner]. [P0371]

Sydney and Fanny Morgan, postman and postmistress at West Alvington. [P1474.1]

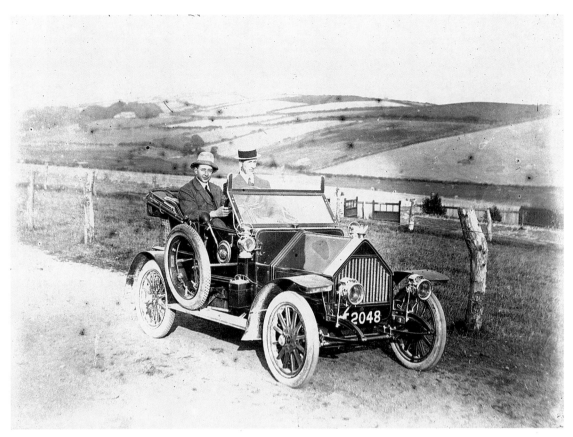

Edward John Tanner and William Stubbs in Mr Tanner's Phoenix car on their way to/from the Links Hotel site in 1910 or 1911. E. J. Tanner was the second person in Kingsbridge to own a car. [Photograph loaned by Mr J. Tanner]

THEN. Twyford House, built by Lt Col Ilbert in 1789 and later occupied by
Colonel Twyford, was by 1902 a private girl's school run by Miss Florence Body.
Until Kingsbridge Grammar School absorbed Twyford School in 1944, this was the
girls' only alternative to the Council School in Fosse Road or boarding school at
Totnes, Newton Abbot or Crediton. However, there were no classrooms available
at the Westville site, so the girls continued to be taught separately in Twyford
House until 1950 when new facilities in the main school site were built. [P0165]

AND NOW. Quay House in 1999, home of Kingsbridge Town Council. [P1537.4]

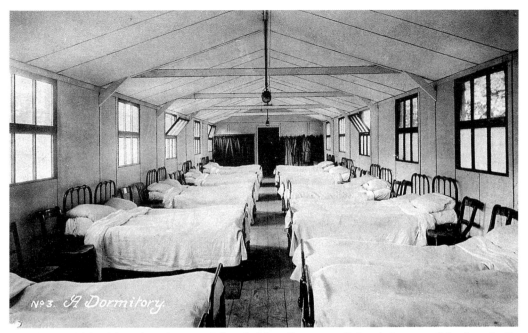

A rather cold-looking dormitory at Kingsbridge Grammar School, in one of the huts built to ease the accommodation problem. [P1376n]

Kingsbridge Grammar School – Third form classroom at 20 Fore Street. A room at the top of the building. The boys were seated in alphabetical order, so those at the front had the modern desks with lift-up lids and seat backs, while those at the back had to suffer the splintered benches in the forefront of this photograph. In 1929-1930 they were Rossiter, Smaridge, Snowdon, Tanner, Taylor, and Windsor. [P1376p]

Kingsbridge Grammar School classroom in the original school building in Fore Street, now the Cookworthy Museum. The headmaster's desk is very prominent. This was later moved to 20 Fore Street, but has been returned to its original place in the museum. [P1317.2]

Pupils and staff of Kingsbridge Grammar School, 1880. Back row: Landells, Bickford, Speer, Ridehalgh, Day, Luscombe, Dr Rankin, Bickford, Mr Sheale, Tucker, Adams. Front row: Parkhouse, Baron, Crimp, Wroth, Squire, Stoneman, Carpenter, Osmond, Ridehalgh, Square, Warren. [P1491.4]

Kingsbridge Grammar School headmaster from 1891 to 1917, the Reverend W. Watson [Wally] playing tennis. [P1376h]

Opening of Kingsbridge Grammar School at Westville [now Kingsbridge Community College] on 25 June 1931 by Sir Henry Lopes, chairman of Devon County Council. Chairman of Devon's Higher Education Committee [Mr C E Pitman] in his opening speech hoped that the catastrophe of making KGS a mixed school would never happen. [P1377.1]

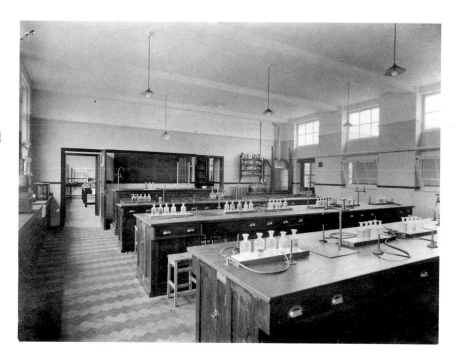

View of science laboratory on opening day in 1931 – state of the art for the time and certainly robust. Similar labs to this were still in use in schools in the late 1970s. [P1377.3]

Kingsbridge Grammar School soccer team 1919-1920. Back row: Mr Smith, Mr Wood, Mr Wykes, J. B. Beringer, G. T. Brown. Middle row: J. Cutler, G. F. Denton, Hector G. Lakeman, H. O. Luscombe, A. J. Irish. Front row: J. W. Maye, C. Phillips, A. D. G. Nosworthy, S. W. A. Gill. [P1375.1]

Kingsbridge Grammar School cricket team circa 1930. Back row: Roper, Ken Oke, Smale, Orchard, Sandercock. Front: Chandler, H. Snowdon, J. A. R. Barnes, Bowerbank, John Mundy, Robinson. [P0489a]

Kingsbridge Senior School 1935, Miss Stone's class. Back row left to right: Mathews, unknown, Ball, Walk, Chope, McCarthy, Langworthy, unknown, Williams, Thomas. Second row: Perkins, Stephens, Holman, Geatches, Head, Cowling, Lakeman, Pengelly, Rendle, James, Ball, Dalton. Third row: Tucker, Jeffery, Solomon, Luscombe, Lethbridge, Collins, Martin, Brooking, Camp, Boon. Front row: Holwill, Spry, Gillard, Morgan, Harvey, Carne, Tucker, Blank, Fawcett. [P1532]

Kingsbridge Senior School woodwork class, 1938, with Mr Crowther. Boon, D. Bolton, B. Cranch, W. Horswill, R. Cope, D. Perring, W. Wilson, Cyril Wood, C. Lethbridge, T. Quick, R. Lethbridge. [P1503.5]

East Portlemouth Primary School, circa 1891. Back row: James Stone, William Powlesland, James Baskerville and J. Elliot. Middle: Mrs Evans [teacher] Miss Emily Powlesland, Lucy, Bert and Jim Jarvis, Eliza Creaber, Francis Stone, Annie Wood, Alice Lamble, Hilda Powlesland [teacher]. Front: William Baskerville, Gladys Wood, Alice Baskerville, Emma Stone, Beat Wotton, Bessie Baskerville, Katie Baskerville, Annie Wotton, Mary Stone, G. Powlesland. [P0970]

Loddiswell Girl Guides, 1930. [P1524.10]

Kingsbridge Brownies circa 1930. [P0502]

Kingsbridge Cubs on field exercise, circa 1932. Boy third from right is Peter Lidstone. [P0506]

Kingsbridge Wolf Cub Pack with home-made rocket life saving apparatus at Kingsbridge, circa 1934. Run by F. E. 'Daddy' Ross, the pack ran from 1923 to 1936, and was disbanded as a result of Devon County Education Committee raising the minimum admission age to boarding schools from eight years to ten years, in 1933. [P1374.1]

Kingsbridge Wolf Cub Pack at Lee Moor in 1934, Head, Burgoyne and Blackler. [P1374.5]

The Proclamation of Edward VII in 1901. Once Kingsbridge Town Hall had been built in 1850, important events were announced from its steps – from the sight of the umbrellas, damp English weather was no excuse to miss the news. [P0207]

Francis Bingham Mildmay, MP for Totnes from 1885 to 1922, addressing the crowds from an upstairs window of the Kings Arms. With no television and little or no radio [the BBC began regular radio broadcasts in 1922], a personal appearance by the local MP was absolutely essential, particularly at election time, as here. Mr Mildmay was highly regarded by the villagers of Hallsands, as he worked tirelessly for years to get some form of compensation for the destruction of the village in 1917. [P0767]

Street party outside the Albion Hotel in Fore Street, probably for Victoria's Diamond Jubilee in 1897. [P0884]

George V Silver Jubilee 1935 – street party in the marketplace at Church Street. [P0384]

Fore Street on 12 May 1937, decorated for George VI's Coronation – showing Tanners, Oke Brothers, Gazette office and Kings Arms. [P0361b]

Kingsbridge carnival 1937 for Coronation of George VI. Uncle Tom Cobley and all consists of: Cyril Hellows, Jack Tanner, Harry Brown, Roy Rossiter, Herbert Pearce, Philip Trant, George Hellas. The horse belonged to Frank Gloynds of Longbrook. [P0034]

VE Day party in Ebrington Street, Kingsbridge, 8 May 1945. [P0075]

Swingboats at fair, circa 1900. [P0570]

British Legion fete at Widdicombe House, 16 July 1936. [P0854.4]

Luscombe family picnic at Slapton Sands in 1890s. Mrs Luscombe is thought to be the lady on the right behind the bucket and spade. [P0901]

Fishing was not only an industry, but a pleasant recreation for some. East Portlemouth, circa 1910. [P0707b]

1922. Kingsbridge Dramatic Society performing 'Tons of Money'. Left to right: Mrs Elsie Adams [nee Blake], Mrs Muriel Grose [nee Balkwill], Mrs Margaret Jinks [nee Donovan], Captain Charles Sadler, Mr W. R. Grose, Mr Osborne. [P0266]

Kingsbridge Bowling Club, Eastern Backway, 1920-24. Back row: Fairweather, M Wingate. Next row: Creed, Webb, Hannaford, Perrott, Lakeman, Horne, Squires, C. B. Head. Middle row: Darke, Green. Front row: Widger, Wyres, Barber, Moysey, Spencer [captain], Staddon, Lamble, Travers, Lang. [P1454]

Beesands Rovers Football Club 1938-1939. Back row: F. Parsliffe, Roper, A. Hatherley. Middle row: N. Brooking, J. Crocker, F. Steer, G .Lamble. Front row: N. Stone, H. Stevens, S. Hutchings, F. Hutchings, B. Rogers. [P1333]

Cricket action at the Butts, West Alvington, 1985. This ground was opened in 1926. [P1208]

Kingsbridge Rugby Football Club Diamond Jubilee celebration for 1889-1949. C. Adams being welcomed by E. Butcher and D. Casely. [P0209]

South Pool Harriers outside the Kings Arms in 1937. [P0377]

Modbury Harriers puppy show on 13 March 1930. [P0393]

Badger hunt at Stadbury, Aveton Gifford, 1921. Participants included Dr Steer, Antony Luscombe, Bill Bowden, Walter Hard, Frank Steer, Edgar Stevans, Fred Lugger [Johnny], and P.C. Sandercock. [P1378.16]

Horses for sale in 1914 on Kingsbridge Quay by the weighbridge. Quay Garage in background, now Wills Marine store. 800 horses were mustered in Kingsbridge alone, for Army selection for training to pull heavy field artillery in France. [P0070]

Kings Own Regiment lined up on Kingsbridge Station circa 1914. [P0590]

1918 Kingsbridge Cadet Corps on War Saving Parade, passing the current Lloyds TSB building. The Cadet Corps was set up in 1918 by Mr P. H. Wykes, headmaster of Kingsbridge Grammar School. [P1376a]

First World War land volunteers, including A. Moore, Mrs Adams, Mrs Wyatt, E. Elliott, B. Browse, Mrs Dobell. [P1369.5]

German POWs from WWI, based in Kingsbridge workhouse, which was built in 1837 at a cost of £6000, to accommodate 350 paupers [not that it ever reached that total]. It is still in use today, although as workshops rather than a workhouse. [P0237]

The US Army D-Day rehearsals in the Slapton area are generally known, but less well-known is the previous exercise by the British army in July 1938 in much the same area, but without the total civilian upheaval. The then-Brigadier Montgomery commanded the 'Eastland' forces, from 'an important industrial country, densely populated', invading the 'Westland', 'a rich agricultural land, whose people, although sturdy and good soldiers, were indolent and easy-going'. The exercise was scheduled to last five days, but stormy weather forced its cancellation after only one, and troops were housed at the Royal Naval College at Dartmouth at extremely short notice, soaking wet and very hungry.

Vickers light tanks, designed by Sir John Cardon, at Slapton Sands for 1938 exercise. [P0843.4]

Mechanised Landing Craft – an early type of landing craft at Slapton Sands, 1938. [P0844.5]

The Royal Sands Hotel in use as headquarters during the 1938 exercise – soldiers, tents, motorbikes, a staff car, wireless truck and 'big ear' are all visible. [P0846.1]

Some of Montgomery's Scots Guards in 1938, 'defending the bridgehead'. [P0847.1]

610 Squadron, Bolt Head, October 1943. A Spitfire squadron engaged in convoy escort duties, bomber escort and offensive patrols, etc. [P1423.9]

Bomb damage in Fore Street, Saturday 2 January 1943. [P1381.2.1]

'When the foundry was hit I came out of the office [Oke Brothers in Bridge Street] and couldn't see anything – just black billowing smoke. My Dad took me home the long way round because Fore Street was bombed too, then he went back to help and found Mrs Lewis. It was ages before they found the two boys who were blown onto the roof. It was lucky for the children that the cinema programme was running late or they would have been in the street when the machine-gunning started. The second raid came on Tuesday, during the funeral of one of the victims of the Saturday raid. The mourners just dropped everything and dived under the pews. By that time there was a gun emplacement on the hill behind Dodbrooke Church, but the planes flew too low for the gun to be any use. The workmen were replacing all the roof-tiles on one house damaged on Saturday and came back after the Tuesday raid to find them all off again.' [Esme Edwards].

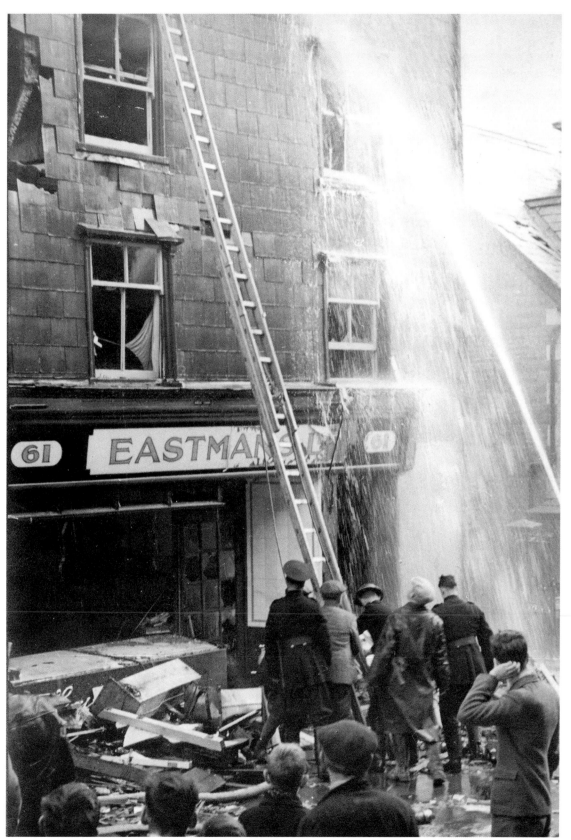

[P1381.2.4]

In August 1943 troops practised a small-scale landing at Slapton Sands, to test its suitability for D-Day training. The Slapton Sands area was considered similar to the beaches which the American forces were scheduled to attack, and so over 3000 residents, 6000 cattle, 12,000 sheep and all the farm equipment were evacuated from their homes in a very wet November-December 1943. It took six weeks to clear an area of twenty five square miles of civilians, their livestock and equipment, and several months to make it safe for their return.

US engineer helping Mr F. Blank of Slapton during 1943 evacuation. [P0872.30]

1943 evacuation. WVS volunteers serving food from a Ministry of Food van which was used to deliver lunches from an emergency kitchen at East Allington. With village shops closing and kitchen equipment transferred to new addresses before the owners, this service was invaluable. [P0872.32]

An emergency kitchen at Strete in 1943 – looks like a barn. Kitchen staff, including Miss K. Goldsmith on the right and Mr Mudd from the Channel Islands behind, preparing a meal for the remaining residents and all those working to clear the area. [P0872.3]

Farm workers moving a threshing machine with a steam tractor in 1943 evacuation. [P0872.43]

Lost dog in Chillington. No traffic, no people, only a lonely dog after the 1943 evacuation was completed. [P0872.24]

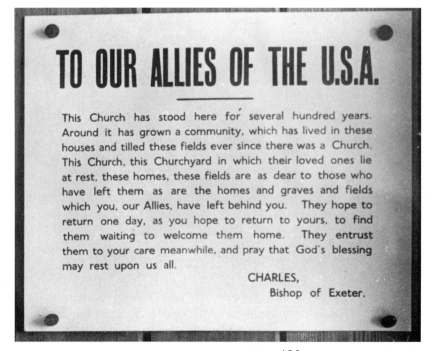

TO OUR ALLIES OF THE U.S.A.

This Church has stood here for several hundred years. Around it has grown a community, which has lived in these houses and tilled these fields ever since there was a Church. This Church, this Churchyard in which their loved ones lie at rest, these homes, these fields are as dear to those who have left them as are the homes and graves and fields which you, our Allies, have left behind you. They hope to return one day, as you hope to return to yours, to find them waiting to welcome them home. They entrust them to your care meanwhile, and pray that God's blessing may rest upon us all.

CHARLES,
Bishop of Exeter.

Notice put up on all church doors in 1943, asking the US soldiers to respect the buildings. From remarks overheard that the British had really gone to town with building this training range, it is apparent that some US soldiers never read this. [P0872.17]

Field Marshal Montgomery and officers passing Ryeford Garage on Kingsbridge Quay, in 1944 when he visited the US Army D-Day exercises. The three excited boys in front of the petrol pumps are Tony Maunder, Michael Pedrick and Michael Gosling. [P1460]

Troops lined up on the Quay for inspection by Field Marshal Montgomery in 1944. [P0558e]

Field Marshal Montgomery at the corner of Bridge Street and Church Street, Kingsbridge in 1944, the centre of an admiring crowd. [P0832.7]

Clearing Fore Street, Kingsbridge, after the blizzard of 1891. [P0039]

The Great Blizzard on 9-10 March 1891 started with hurricane force winds. The winds dropped on Tuesday but the snow continued to fall. Salcombe was cut off from Monday evening until Friday. Coaches couldn't run to Kingsbridge Road Station at Wrangaton, and the navvies building the railway to Kingsbridge helped to clear the roads.

The 1891 blizzard aftermath – rooftops on the northwest side of Fore Street, Kingsbridge. Westville can be seen in the distance as an isolated group of houses. [P0551]

1891 blizzard. Two men in a sailing boat breaking the ice on the estuary. [P0931]

30 December 1927 snow blizzard. Nearly fifty men were needed to clear the road between Aveton Gifford and Kingsbridge. The Beechwood food van was the first vehicle to get through to Churchstow after the blizzard. [P0389]

Passengers disembarking from the paddle steamer Kenwith Castle at New Quay, Kingsbridge, in November 1927. This was the only means of travel to and from Salcombe for the best part of a week. [P1483]

Slapton Ley froze hard enough in 1939 for all sorts of activities to take place – skating, sliding and even a tea party – although the surface was hardly ice-rink smooth. Seated in the middle is Miss Hill, owner of Torcross Hotel. Bill Turner, handyman at the hotel is standing to the left with Bob Pearce, head waiter, to the right. Mrs Elsie Beer is seated far right. [P0836.17.1]

The winter of 1945-6 with snow on the beach at Torcross. [P0836.15.4]

Sir John Jackson, owner of the dredging company, insisted the shingle would return following dredging in the early 1900s. This was not the case and the full extent of the damage became apparent over the following years, culminating in the destruction of Hallsands in 1917 as shown. [P0247]

London Inn, Hallsands – the collapsed extension was built on compacted sand between rock clefts, unlike the rest of the inn which was built on solid rock. When the sea breached the defences it sucked out the sand foundations, and those houses in Hallsands which were built on this type of surface were the first to collapse. [P0878]

Torcross. Storm damage in 1951 and 1979, and more recently in 2001, have led to the construction of various sea defences here and at Beesands. The gravel dredging of the late 1890s which exposed Hallsands is commonly blamed for the vulnerability of this part of the coastline. The 1978-9 storm combined severe gale force easterly winds with very high spring tides. [P1359.2]

Salcombe flood 1925. High tides often flooded Fore Street from Customs Quay to Kings Arms Quay. This was partly cured by raising the level of the road. [P1400.4.5]

1925. Clifton Place, Salcombe, flooded at high tide. [P1400.3.14]

1925. Fore Street, Salcombe flooded at high tide. [P0129]

Bridge Street, Kingsbridge, flooded at high tide – an unwelcome but still familiar sight, as even now the street has been known to flood on spring tides. The owners of the King of Prussia admitted defeat some years ago and removed the carpets rather than keep replacing them. [P0255]

'The Marsh', now the recreation ground on Kingsbridge embankment, in 1924. The house was Fox Hall, once the home of the Trant family of the Town Mill, and formerly officers' quarters when soldiers were based here. [P0253.3]

Kingsbridge recreation ground flooded in 1960. The schoolboy on the left is Fred Dennis. Bus station and Rack Park estate in background. [P1336.3]

The rare tidal phenomenon of an incoming tide on two sides of the natural causeway at Bigbury Bay was used to great effect in the Kirk Douglas film 'Holocaust 2000'. The large garages visible on the mainland were filled with the cars of hotel guests. [P0495]